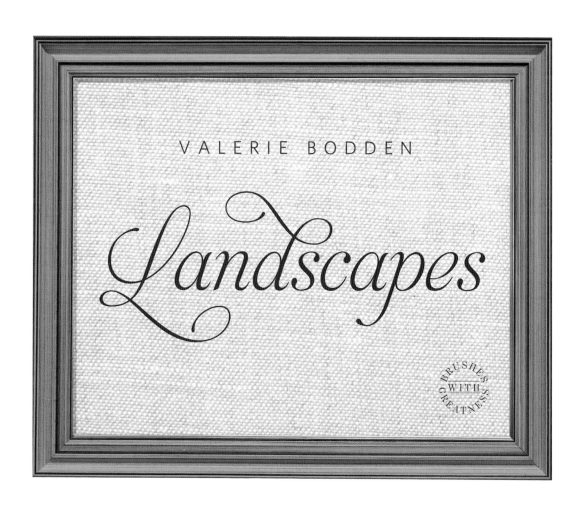

VALERIE BODDEN

Landscapes

BRUSHES WITH GREATNESS

CREATIVE EDUCATION

Published by Creative Education P.O. Box 227, Mankato, Minnesota 56002
Creative Education is an imprint of The Creative Company www.thecreativecompany.us

Design and production by Liddy Walseth Art direction by Rita Marshall
Printed in the United States of America

Photographs by Alamy (Tomas Abad, The Art Gallery Collection, Lebrecht Music and Arts Photo Library), Artists Rights
Society (© 2012 Artists Rights Society (ARS), New York/VG Bild-Kunst, Bonn), Art Resource (Alinari, Erich Lessing, Terra
Foundation for American Art, The Museum of Modern Art/Licensed by SCALA), The Bridgeman Art Library (Fenollosa-Weld
Collection, Alinari, Pushkin Museum, Moscow, Russia/Giraudon), Corbis (Alexander Burkatovski), Getty Images (Giotto di
Bondone, Buyenlarge/Buyenlarge/Time Life Pictures, John Constable/The Bridgeman Art Library, Dorling Kindersley, Guy
Gillette, Ernst Haas/Hulton Archive, French School, Hulton Archive, Kean Collection, SuperStock, Vincent van Gogh, Kirk
Wilkinson/Pix Inc./Time Life Pictures), iStockphoto (ChrisAt, Yanik Chauvin, Deanna Finn, Konstantin Kirillov, Erik Lam,
Josef Muellek), Shutterstock (Subbotina Anna, Jakub Krechowicz, Chris Pole), SuperStock (The Art Archive, Bridgeman Art
Library, Fine Art Images), The Rubell Family Collection, Wikipedia (Paul Cezanne, Katsushika Hokusai)

Library of Congress Cataloging-in-Publication Data
Bodden, Valerie.
Landscapes / by Valerie Bodden.
p. cm. — (Brushes with greatness)
Includes bibliographical references and index.
Summary: A survey of the painting genre that focuses on landforms and elements of nature, examining the genre's origins
and introducing its notable artists, works, and styles throughout history.
ISBN 978-1-60818-201-5
1. Landscape painting. I. Title.
ND1340.B63 2012
758'.1—dc23   2011040487

First edition

2 4 6 8 9 7 5 3 1

COVER: *THATCHED COTTAGES* (1890), BY VINCENT
VAN GOGH PAGE 2: DETAIL OF *WHEATFIELD WITH
REAPER* (1889), BY VAN GOGH

TABLE OF CONTENTS

CHAPTERS

4	THE LANDSCAPE BACKGROUND
16	INTO THE FOREGROUND
26	EXPERIMENTAL LANDSCAPING
37	CHANGING LANDSCAPES FOR A CHANGING TIME

APPRECIATING ART

15	*ST. FRANCIS IN THE DESERT*
25	*THE GREAT WAVE AT KANAGAWA*
35	*MONT SAINTE-VICTOIRE SEEN FROM THE*
	BIBÉMUS QUARRY
45	*CHRISTINA'S WORLD*

RESOURCES

46	GLOSSARY
47	SELECTED BIBLIOGRAPHY
48	INDEX

the Landscape Background

ALTHOUGH VISITORS TO AN ART MUSEUM TODAY MIGHT THINK NOTHING OF SEEING NUMEROUS LANDSCAPE PAINTINGS ON EXHIBIT, the idea of a work of art depicting only the natural world, with no human or **divine** figures, was once radical. It was not until the 1500s that landscape was recognized as a legitimate painting **genre** in the **West**. Since that time, landscape painting has helped push the progress of artistic developments, moving from idealized to realistic, expressionistic, and even **abstract** views of the natural world.

The flourishing art scene of the ancient Greek world revolved around the human figure in both sculpture and painting. Beginning around the first century B.C., however, landscape painting flowered briefly in the form of wall paintings and frescoes (paintings made on walls using watercolors on wet plaster). These frescoes were found in the homes of wealthy Romans and may actually have been copies of Greek wall paintings created 100 or 200 years earlier. According to the Roman scholar Pliny (A.D. 23–79), Roman wall paintings depicted "country houses, colonnades, garden structures, groves, forests, hills, ponds, seas, rivers, shores, whatever one wished."

Landscape painting prevailed in Rome until about the fourth century A.D. By the end of that century, however, the Roman Empire—which controlled most of Europe, northern Africa, and the Middle East—was split into the western Roman Empire and the eastern Roman Empire, also known as the Byzantine Empire. By the fifth century, the western empire had fallen, and Europe entered a period known as the Middle Ages, which lasted nearly 1,000 years. During this time, the Catholic Church exerted strong influence throughout most of Europe, and religious subjects, including stories from the Bible and legends about saints, were regarded as the proper focus of artwork. That artwork was usually in the form of wall or altar paintings, **mosaics**, or tapestries in cathedrals and churches. Some

DETAIL FROM THE *MAESTÀ ALTARPIECE* (1308-11, OPPOSITE), BY ITALIAN DUCCIO DI BUONINSEGNA; DETAIL FROM *THE ANNUNCIATION* (C. 1305, ABOVE), BY GIOTTO DI BONDONE

small paintings illustrated the pages of **illuminated manuscripts** as well.

During the early Middle Ages, artistic achievement reached its greatest heights in the Byzantine Empire. In order to emphasize the spiritual aspects of religion, many Byzantine artists rejected realistic portrayals in favor of flat images with strong lines and rich colors. Landscapes appeared only in the background, where they served as **symbols**. A lily, for example, was not simply a plant but a representation of the **Virgin Mary**'s purity. Such symbols were often highly **stylized**, varying little from one painting to the next, and rarely gave an illusion of space or reality. By the later Middle Ages, the Byzantine style had spread to Italy and other parts of Europe.

While European art revolved around

Christian subjects during the Middle Ages, in China, where nature was viewed as sacred, landscapes began to emerge as the subjects of their own paintings around the sixth century A.D. Many Chinese artists spent years in remote natural retreats where they observed nature. They later made pictures of it from memory, often in monochromatic (single-color) inks. Although the images often appeared realistic, most were compilations of scenes the artist had put together in order to create an idealized, spiritual representation of nature. Each aspect of a painting generally had symbolic meaning. Clouds stood for changeability, for example. The artist attempted to capture a mood or feeling, which might also be expressed through a poem inked on the scene. Contact between China and Japan led to the Japanese adoption of Chinese painting styles in the seventh and eighth centuries. By the 12th century, however, Japanese artists had developed their own style, known as Yamato-e (*YAH-mah-toh-WEH*), using vivid colors to create flat pictures of native literature or the seasons.

As landscape continued to be the focus of art in the East, Western art was beginning to undergo its own

transformation. The highly stylized, formulaic portrayal of nature common to the Middle Ages slowly gave way to a more naturalistic view. This change was sparked largely by Italian artist Giotto di Bondone (c. 1266–1337), whose frescoes and altarpieces focused on religious subjects. Although Giotto's landscapes remained relatively flat and in the background of his pictures, they served as more than mere decoration or symbol; the natural world became part of the picture's story. Instead of taking his landscapes directly from nature, Giotto carefully composed his pictures, placing each element in the most logical position.

Giotto is often considered a forerunner of the Renaissance. Beginning in the 1400s in Italy and spreading across Europe, the Renaissance marked a revival of interest in the classical art and culture of the ancient Greeks and Romans. In art, the Renaissance was characterized by a continued focus on the human figure in the form of religious or classical narratives, or stories. At the same time, though, many painters began to pay more attention to the natural world. Landscape gained importance, taking up more of the picture space and being presented in a more natural form, even though artists still followed formal rules for composition, making sure that their works were balanced and **symmetrical**.

The early Renaissance painter Masaccio (1401–28), from Florence, was one of the first to present his religious figures in a realistic **contemporary** setting rather than an imagined past. He gave depth to his works with the newly developed technique of **linear perspective**. Later Renaissance artists such as Leonardo da Vinci (1452–1519) also used this technique. Da Vinci further contributed to the illusion of depth by making objects in the distance appear

blue and blurred. He spent much time in the scientific observation of nature and suggested that young artists sketch outdoors and then use their sketches as the basis for finished paintings created in their studios.

Meanwhile, in northern Europe, Renaissance painters from **Flanders** and the Netherlands used light and color to unify their works and create a feeling of depth. They accurately depicted even the tiniest details, down to leaves and shadows, and painted biblical stories and **secular** myths in settings designed to enhance the message of the work. Even these realistic landscapes often still had symbolic meaning, however.

Although religious art dominated from the Middle Ages through the Renaissance in Europe, landscapes were

portrayed in other types of works as well. Many wealthy landowners, for example, requested landscapes to document their landholdings, and some artists used their talents to create images of an earthly paradise or a golden age of the past. Such paintings, beautiful as they might be, were typically considered inferior to figurative or narrative art.

By the early 16th century, though, prominent painters in both the Netherlands and Italy had begun to allow the landscape to dominate their pictures, reducing human figures to an almost incidental part of the painting. The work of northern artists was distinguished by an increasing focus on naturalism, while Italians began to concentrate

THE LAST SUPPER (1495–98), BY LEONARDO DA VINCI

more on the use of color and light to create poetic moods and ideal landscapes. This difference was influenced in part by differing painting methods, as Italian artists had to work quickly to finish their frescoes before they dried, while northern European artists began to use oil paints, which dried slowly, allowing them to labor over every detail.

The early years of the 16th century also brought about the first pure landscapes, unpopulated by figures, created by artists from Germany and Flanders. Although these landscapes did not tell a story, they still held meaning for viewers, who regarded them as a reflection of God's glory. Soon, paintings in which landscape dominated were in high demand among Italian princes and collectors, and by the end of the century, landscape was at last widely recognized as a proper subject for painting in and of itself.

ULYSSES AND CIRCE (C. 1580), BY ITALIAN ALESSANDRO ALLORI

APPRECIATING ART

St. Francis in the Desert (c. 1480)

Giovanni Bellini, Italian (c. 1430–1516)

49 x 55-7/8 inches (124.5 x 141.9 cm)

In this painting, Bellini depicts St. Francis standing in awe as he views the power of God in nature. Although the sun cannot be seen in the picture, its golden light warms the scene, spreading over the town in the background hills, the fields, and the gray-green rocks where St. Francis stands in front of his cave. Bellini employed the new medium of oil paints, along with **tempera** paints, applying thin layers of **pigment** in order to achieve subtle lighting effects. The clear light shining on the scene illuminates every detail, revealing a dedication to naturalistic representation in everything from leaves to rocks.

The use of color enables Bellini to create a realistic feeling of depth in this picture. St. Francis seems to be one with the natural world that surrounds him. The tree at the left edge of the scene bends gently toward him, while the rock on which he stands offers a natural stage to support him. Like most Renaissance artists, Bellini has incorporated a number of symbols into his image. The grape arbor marking the entrance to the saint's cave was a symbol of the Christian sacrament of Holy Communion, and water pouring out of a spout in the rock is a reference to the Old Testament prophet Moses, who struck a rock to release water in the desert. The entire scene evokes a sense of holiness in the portrayal of nature—and the viewer is invited to share in the awe experienced by the saint.

Into The Foreground

WELL BEFORE LANDSCAPE HAD BECOME A LEGITIMATE SUBJECT FOR PAINTING, Italian artist Ambrogio Lorenzetti (c. 1285–c. 1348) had painted the first scene taken directly from real life. Instead of portraying religious subjects, Lorenzetti focused on the secular world in a series of frescoes on the walls of the Palazzo Pubblico, a government building in the city of Siena, in central Italy. In one fresco, *Effects of Good Government on Town and Country* (1337–39), Lorenzetti presents a realistic, though probably not exact, view of the countryside around Siena, with its orchards, fields, and terraces. Although the 23-foot-long (7 m) fresco includes figures, the landscape is the true subject of the picture. The figures that dot the countryside are simple peasants carrying out their work of plowing, sowing, hunting, and traveling through the land.

Lorenzetti's focus on landscape was unique for his time, and it wasn't until the Renaissance of the 15th and 16th centuries that other artists began to give

THE VIRGIN AND CHILD WITH CHANCELLOR ROLIN, BY JAN VAN EYCK

THE TEMPEST, BY GIORGIONE

more attention to the portrayal of landscapes. Although Jan van Eyck (c. 1390–c. 1441), of Flanders, painted religious scenes, he included in them extensive landscape backgrounds. In *The Virgin and Child with Chancellor Rolin* (1435), for example, Mary presents Jesus to Nicolas Rolin, a government official, in a luxurious residence. But the viewer's eye is drawn past the figures to the sunlit landscape beyond, complete with gardens, a river, rolling hills, and distant mountains. One of the first artists to experiment with oil paints (in place of tempera), van Eyck worked slowly, placing one layer of pigment on top of another, which allowed him to convey a sense of depth through the subtle play of light over the picture. This technique, known as atmospheric perspective, soon became a hallmark of Flemish artists (artists from Flanders).

In Italy, Giorgione (c. 1477–c. 1510) was one of the first artists to be referred to as a landscape painter, despite the fact that his paintings always included either secular or religious figures. These figures appear in the foreground but are often small in scale compared with the picture space devoted to the landscape. The use of color helped to bring unity to Giorgione's paintings and to establish a specific mood. In *The Tempest* (c. 1505–09), the artist uses color to create a feeling of mystery and tension, with dark storm clouds broken only by a bright bolt of lightning. The unexplained figures of a soldier and a woman nursing her child, illuminated in the foreground of the imaginative scene, have long made the interpretation of this picture a topic of speculation for scholars. Whatever their meaning, the figures seem almost to retreat into the landscape, adding to the scene's sense of mystery and poetry.

Working around the same time as Giorgione, German artist Albrecht Altdorfer (c. 1480–1538) painted what is considered to be the first Western landscape without figures. His *Danube Landscape near Regensburg* (c. 1522–25) portrays a road through a forest leading to a castle and distant mountains. Although the work gives a fairly realistic portrayal of the scenery found near the Danube River, Altdorfer was more concerned with portraying the effects of light, especially on clouds and foliage. Altdorfer did include figures in many of his works, but they were often eclipsed by the surrounding landscape. In *St. George* and the Dragon (1510), for example, the saint and his horse are nearly swallowed by the untamed forest. Altdorfer's landscapes made him a primary figure of the Danube school, a group of artists who painted around the Danube River valley in Germany and Austria and whose works were characterized by expressions of nature's power.

Altdorfer's contemporary, Flemish painter Joachim Patinir (c. 1485–1524) also allowed landscape to dominate his pictures and overshadow his figures, to such an extent that German painter Albrecht Dürer (1471–1528) referred to him as "the good landscape painter." Although Patinir's works portray religious scenes, they are set in encompassing landscapes, often viewed from above. In order to achieve a sense of depth, Patinir relied on color and atmosphere in place of linear perspective. In Landscape with the Flight into Egypt (1516–17), the tiny figures of Mary, Joseph, and Jesus climb brown cliffs in the foreground. Behind them, the city of Bethlehem stands among green fields. In the far distance are blue-tinged forests, mountains, water, and sky.

Patinir's style soon spread from Germany to Italy, where demand for paintings inspired by his work was high among collectors. As a result, many artists of the north began to specialize in landscape painting. One such artist was Pieter Bruegel the Elder (c. 1525–69) of Flanders, whom Flemish geographer Abraham Ortelius (1527–98) praised as "nature among painters." Many of Bruegel's landscapes presented scenes of rural peasant life. In a series of six landscapes known as The Seasons, Bruegel's portrayal of peasant figures is overshadowed by his focus on changes in weather, from the golden warmth of summer in Haymaking (1565) to the icy-white cold of winter in Hunters in the Snow (1565). Visible brushstrokes enhance the particular atmosphere of each seasonal picture.

By the 1600s, European art had entered a period that came to be known as the Baroque. Although Baroque art varied widely from country to country and artist to artist, in almost all cases, it was characterized by the use of light to convey emotion. French Baroque artist Claude Lorrain (1600–82), who painted in Italy, spent hours working outdoors, making oil sketches of the play of light over the land. Yet his finished works do not come directly from nature. He took his sketches back to the studio to compose a final work based on the classical order found in ancient Greek art, using trees

THE HARVESTERS
(1565), BY PIETER
BRUEGEL THE ELDER

or classical buildings to frame the scene. His "perfected," or idealized, landscapes eliminated anything unappealing or disorderly. Lorrain's final compositions benefitted from his outdoor studies of light, as his scenes were often bathed in the golden glow of sunset or the blue haze of sunrise, lending a feeling of poetic beauty and calm to the landscapes. The warm light of his *Seaport with the Embarkation of Saint Ursula* (1641), for example, unifies the picture, drawing attention from the figures in the foreground to the open sea beyond.

Dutch master Jacob van Ruisdael (c. 1628–82) created Baroque works with an entirely different feeling, using light and shadow to convey a mood of mystery or grandeur. In *The Jewish Cemetery* (c. 1654–55), a hidden light shines through gathering storm clouds, casting a sense of melancholy over the tombs and wild shrubbery. In many of his works, van Ruisdael also incorporated another Dutch innovation—a low horizon, which allowed

the sky to fill much of the picture space. In *View of Haarlem* (c. 1675), for example, realistic-looking clouds fill nearly two-thirds of the canvas.

In contrast to the realism of such European paintings, 17th-century Japanese artist Tawaraya Sōtatsu (active c. 1600–40) created simplified pictures that offered a suggestion, rather than a realistic picture, of the natural world. By reducing or eliminating ink outlines and applying one pigment on top of another, still wet pigment, Sōtatsu produced pictures dominated by large regions of bright, overlapping colors. His *Waves at Matsushima* (c. 1624–44), for example, features islands made up of bold patches of green, blue, and brown that blend into one another as gold and white waves swirl around the points of land.

WAVES AT MATSUSHIMA, BY TAWARAYA SŌTATSU

APPRECIATING ART

The Great Wave at Kanagawa (c. 1831–33)

Katsushika Hokusai, Japanese (1760–1849)

10-1/8 x 14-15/16 inches (25.7 x 37.9 cm)

This work comes from a series of woodblock prints designed by Hokusai, entitled *Thirty-Six Views of Mount Fuji*. In order to create the print, Hokusai first made a sketch of the scene, which was then attached to several blocks of wood. The wood was carved away by an engraver to create a **relief** of the image. Each woodblock was then painted with a separate ink color and pressed onto a sheet of paper to make the final print.

Hokusai's pictures of Mount Fuji are in the ukiyo-e (Japanese for "pictures of the floating world") style of printmaking common in 17th- through 19th-century Japanese art. As a careful student of many types of art, including European, Hokusai learned the technique of perspective and adapted it to his own prints. In *The Great Wave at Kanagawa*, the snow-capped Mount Fuji lies far in the distance, dwarfed by a huge ocean wave in the foreground. The bold, curving lines of the wave rise toward the sky, about to break over the boats below, creating a feeling of expectation and tension. In the foreground, a smaller wave mimics the shape and color of Mount Fuji. The sky appears to be lit by the sun despite the storm clouds. The image is not naturalistic but stylistic, focusing on line and bold patches of color rather than on creating an accurate imitation of nature. The print is one of Hokusai's most famous works and has been highly admired, especially in the West, where its simplified forms had a strong influence on late 19th-century art.

Experimental Landscaping

DURING THE EARLY YEARS OF THE 18TH CENTURY, artists in France began to create works in the graceful, delicate style known as Rococo. Rococo paintings often presented mythical or courtly scenes in light, airy settings. *Pilgrimage to Cythera* (1717) by French artist Jean-Antoine Watteau (1684–1721) provides a poetic glimpse of young people on the mythical island of Cythera, also known as the "island of love," rendered in soft pastel shades. The Rococo style flourished until about the middle of the 1700s, when it was rejected as too frivolous and replaced by a movement called Neoclassicism—a return to the idealized, orderly style of classical Greek and Roman art and to historical subject matter.

Around the same time, however, another group of artists began to look at the natural world differently. Rather than finding beauty only in the idealized, logical view of nature offered by Neoclassical works, these artists recognized the value of the untamed wilderness, and many turned their focus to painting the sublime, or awe-inspiring, elements of nature, such as dramatic storms or rocky cliffs. Their goal was to appeal to the emotions and, especially, to arouse feelings of wonder or fear in the viewer. By the end of the century, this new focus on the wild and emotions had come together in the Romantic Movement.

The Romantic Movement's focus

AN EMBARRASSING PROPOSAL (1719, ABOVE), BY JEAN-ANTOINE WATTEAU; *LANDSCAPE WITH WATERFALL* (C. 1714, LEFT), BY WATTEAU

on nature brought landscape painting to the forefront of the artistic world for the first time. German Romantic painter Caspar David Friedrich (1774–1840) made careful studies of nature, but he set his sketches aside when it was time to paint his final work. His aim was to present not an accurate view of the natural world but rather an emotional and even spiritual response to it. He believed that an artist should paint not only "what he sees before him, but also what he sees inside himself." In paintings such as *Monk by the Sea* (1809), Friedrich emphasizes humankind's insignificance in the face of the vastness of creation. In the work, a lone, tiny figure stands on a small strip of shoreline, gazing out upon a dark, imposing sea and an oppressive, low-hanging sky. The only signs of life other than the monk are a few gulls almost hidden in the clouds.

Not all Romantic works emphasized the overpowering force of nature, though. Some, such as those of English painter John Constable (1776–1837), brought a new passion to quiet scenes of the open countryside. Constable spent long hours outdoors, creating oil sketches from nature and closely observing the sky, which he

referred to as "the key note" of a painting. Back in his studio, Constable created his final paintings—some more than six feet (1.8 m) wide and four feet (1.2 m) tall—using thick paint often applied with a palette knife. His most famous painting, *The Hay Wain* (1821), was one such "six-footer," depicting a realistic view of the English countryside near his boyhood home of Suffolk. Rich textures characterize trees, fields, and the walls of a cottage, while the changing light is revealed in both the bright, true-to-life clouds and their reflection in the stream below.

Meanwhile, across the Atlantic Ocean, Romantic landscape painting was beginning to take shape on a new continent as well, as English-born American painter Thomas Cole (1801–48) founded the Hudson River school. Taking their name from the river valley that inspired much of their work, the Hudson River artists were enthralled with the American wilderness. Their fascination can be seen in Cole's *The Oxbow* (1836), which portrays a bend in the Connecticut River. On one side of the river, the land is orderly and cultivated. On the other, it is

THE HAY WAIN, BY JOHN CONSTABLE

overgrown, wild, and mysteriously shrouded in storm clouds.

By Cole's time, centuries' worth of artists had spent their days observing and sketching nature outdoors. Until the 1800s, however, they had completed their final works in the studio. But in the 1820s, premixed jars (and later tubes) of oil paint became available, making it possible for artists to easily take their paints outside. Among the first groups of artists to paint finished works *en plein air* (French for "in the open air") were the Impressionists of France, whose goal was to capture the effects of light, shadow, and color to create an "impression" of nature. They worked quickly, covering their canvases with strong, choppy brushstrokes of bright colors. Some even went so far as to eliminate black and gray from their palettes, painting shadows in color. Impressionist painters also did away with solid outlines and carefully defined forms, allowing objects to subtly blend into their surroundings instead.

The leader of the Impressionists was Claude Monet (1840–1926), whose *Impression, Sunrise* (1873) gave the group its name. In the painting, which pictures the harbor of Le Havre, color has become more important than the subject matter— the place—itself. Strong horizontal brushstrokes of blue and orange create an impression of light reflecting off the water. Monet was so interested in the effects of light that he often made a series of paintings based on the same subject viewed under different lighting conditions, as in his series of wheat stacks painted in 1890 and 1891, including *Stack of Wheat (Sunset, Snow Effect)*, *Stack of Wheat (End of Day, Autumn)*, and *Stack of Wheat (End of Summer)*.

For a time, Dutch painter Vincent van Gogh (1853–90), who moved to France in 1886, experimented with the techniques of the Impressionists. He found, however, that Impressionism prevented him from expressing his deepest emotions. Van Gogh turned to bright, contrasting colors and sharp, broken strokes and swirls of paint to convey his feelings. His belief

CLAUDE MONET, PICTURED LATE IN LIFE

IMPRESSION, SUNRISE,
BY MONET

HARVEST IN PROVENCE (1888),
BY VINCENT VAN GOGH

that "color expresses something in itself" can be seen in landscape paintings such as *Harvest in Provence* (1888), in which bright yellow fields evoke a sense of energy and life. By contrast, one of his final paintings, *Wheatfield with Crows* (1890), with its dark sky pressing down on an over-bright, yellow field, reveals the inner torment of the artist, who would soon commit suicide. According to a letter from van Gogh to his brother, the wheat field in this and other late works was his attempt "to express sadness, extreme loneliness."

Like van Gogh, the school of painters known as *Les Fauves* (French for "the wild beasts") sought to express themselves through color. In place of the despair so often felt in van Gogh's works, Fauvists used pure, bright pigments to convey a sense of delight and joy. In fact, one of the best-known works of the movement, by French artist Henri Matisse (1869–1954), is entitled *Joy of Life* (1905–06). On this large canvas, Matisse uses simplified, curving outlines and large patches of bright color—yellow and purple grass, orange and green trees, and pink sky—to present a new and unique vision of paradise, complete with sparsely detailed nude forms lounging and dancing across the landscape.

While Matisse and other landscape painters continued to focus on color, other artists began to experiment with form, leading to the development of Cubism by Spanish-born painter Pablo Picasso (1881–1973) and French artist Georges Braque (1882–1963), both of whom worked in Paris. Cubists did not attempt to render depth or perspective but instead took objects apart and reassembled them as flat "cubes," or fragments. In Picasso's *House in a Garden* (1908–09) and Braque's *Houses at L'Estaque* (1908), for example, the painters have simplified the forms of houses and trees into fragmented blocks. The sparse use of color helps to strengthen the focus on structure and form.

APPRECIATING ART

Mont Sainte-Victoire Seen from the Bibémus Quarry (c. 1897)

Paul Cézanne, French (1839–1906)

25-1/2 x 32 inches (64.8 x 81.3 cm)

Cézanne initially exhibited with the Impressionists, but by the time he created this work, he had turned away from Impressionism to create his own style. Although he continued to paint outdoors like the Impressionists, Cézanne worked slowly, painstakingly seeking to capture not a fleeting moment but the "bones of nature," or the solid structure hidden beneath the surface of natural objects.

Cézanne made at least 60 paintings of Mont Sainte-Victoire, a mountain peak in southern France. Although many of the works pictured the mountain from a distance, in *Mont Sainte-Victoire Seen from the Bibémus Quarry*, the artist brings the viewer close to the peak, which looms above us across a steep quarry. Disregarding perspective, Cézanne has made objects in the distance larger than those in the foreground, thereby flattening the picture space. What sense of depth there is is created by the use of color. The vertical lines of the quarry, the trees, and the mountain, unrelieved by horizontal planes, direct the eyes upward, toward the mountain's peak at the top of the canvas. Bold outlines and strong blocks of pure color present not an accurate representation of the scene, but rather a feeling of the solidity of the mountain. Bright oranges, greens, and blues help to unify the foreground and background. Cézanne's use of color and space had a tremendous impact on the development of 20th-century art and exercised a direct influence on both Cubism and Fauvism. In fact, Cubist Pablo Picasso and Fauvist Henri Matisse are alternately credited as having called Cézanne "the father of us all."

SAILS (1911), BY ARTHUR G. DOVE

Changing Landscapes for Changing Times

THROUGHOUT THE LATE 1800S, landscape painting dominated the art world as artists experimented with painterly techniques and subject matter. Although landscape lost some of its dominance during the 20th century as many artists turned to new forms of artistic expression, those landscapes that were created reflected a continued emphasis on experimentation. Artists working within a number of new styles and schools—such as abstraction, Surrealism, and photorealism—presented their own, often widely differing, views of the natural world.

Continuing the focus on form begun by the Cubists and other early 20th-century painters, abstract artists emphasized color, line, and texture, eliminating recognizable content or subject matter from their works. Abstract art, though not depicting objects in and of themselves, was at times based on views of the natural world. It presented not a picture of a scene but an *idea* of a scene. American artist Arthur G. Dove (1880–1946) was among the first in the U.S. to create abstract art, yet his pictures were not wholly without content. He based the form of his paintings on natural objects, such as sand barges. The objects are so changed in form,

recognizable elements, depicted with great detail, but these elements might be distorted or put together in bizarre, illogical ways. Surrealists created wildly differing works yet remained united by their focus on the subconscious. Some, such as Spanish painter Salvador Dali (1904–89), created wide, bleak—and at times startlingly realistic—landscapes populated by bizarre or deformed objects. In contrast, Belgian painter René Magritte (1898–1967) focused on the problems of human perception, creating several works in which a landscape painting blocks part of a window. Viewers wonder—but never know—whether the painting depicts the actual view out the window, raising questions about the difference between illusion and reality.

however, as to be unrecognizable until one reads the title of the work, after which the rolling forms of a landscape may be detected.

Begun in part as a reaction against abstract art's focus on form, Surrealist painters emphasized the content of their pictures, creating landscapes that, on first glance, might appear real, but on closer examination are logically impossible. According to "The Surrealist Manifesto," a document published in 1924, the goal of Surrealism was to unite the worlds of reality and dreams in "an absolute reality, a surreality." In order to do this, some Surrealists relied on automatic painting, a technique in which they painted whatever came into their mind, trying to reveal their **subconscious** thoughts. Surrealist paintings often contained

During World War II (1939–45), many European Surrealist painters fled to the U.S., where their techniques of automatic painting helped to inspire the development of Abstract Expressionism. This new movement, which made America the center of the art world for the first time, emphasized abstract works as a means of emotional expression. Some Abstract Expressionists, such as American Jackson Pollock (1912–56), smeared, splattered, poured, dragged, or scraped their paint across large canvases in ways that they

SALVADOR DALI
(OPPOSITE); *THE
FONT* (1930, ABOVE),
BY DALI

MOUNTAINS AND SEA, BY HELEN FRANKENTHALER

FRANKENTHALER AT WORK IN 1969

felt were exciting or mysterious, seeking to evoke a mood rather than a specific image. Often that mood recalled the energy of a landscape painting. In other works, such as the vast color fields of American Mark Rothko (1903–70), some critics saw a new interpretation of the American landscape despite the fact that Rothko insisted, "There is no landscape in my work." In contrast, American Abstract Expressionist Helen Frankenthaler (1928– 2011) gave some of her works landscape titles, such as the brightly colored *Mountains and Sea* (1952).

In the 1960s and '70s, other artists who were known as environmental or land artists left the canvas behind and began to work with the land itself, turning natural landscapes into art. Their goal was to send a message about humans'

relation to the natural world and the connection between art and life. In one large "earthwork," for example, American artist Robert Smithson (1938–73) created a 1,500-foot-long (457 m) spiral of earth and rock in Utah's Great Salt Lake, entitling the work *Spiral Jetty* (1970). The work remains today, although it is often covered by water. Other artists created smaller, less permanent forms of Earth Art. British artist Andy Goldsworthy (1956–) once created a work called *Maple Leaf Lines* (1987), in which he arranged red maple leaves in a shallow stream. Unlike *Spiral Jetty*, *Maple Leaf Lines* is long since gone, but its record lives on in photographs.

Photographs also played an important role in the development of a new, super-realistic style of painting known as photorealism, which began in the U.S. in the 1960s and '70s as a reaction against Abstract Expressionism and spread throughout Europe in the following decades. Rather than looking to nature as their inspiration, photorealists based their works on photographs. Their goal was to freeze an instant in a photograph and then to painstakingly recreate every detail of that image in paint, making it nearly impossible to distinguish the painting from the original photograph.

In fact, they often used the photographs themselves to aid in making their pictures, either by dividing the photo into a series of gridlines and then reproducing the work on their canvas or by projecting a slide of the photographic image onto their canvas and then **airbrushing** over the image, usually making it larger than the original photograph. At times, photorealists distorted certain elements of their paintings in order to direct the viewer's attention to a specific detail or image or to question the nature of reality. While photorealists often painted portraits and still lifes, many also turned to landscape, usually depicting the urban world rather than focusing on rural scenery. *Lee (Corner Window)* (1974) by American artist Richard Estes (1932–), for example, presents a city view as reflected in the glass of a store window, including the distortions caused by that reflected view.

In the 21st century, some artists

took photorealism further to create "hyperrealism," in which they worked from digital images to create works that looked like high-definition photographs. Textures and shadows were even more defined than in the digital images themselves, and the artists often brought out details that could not be seen by the naked eye, creating a "new" reality. Unlike photorealists, many hyperrealists sought to convey a subtle message or feeling through their work.

The early 21st century also saw the emergence of the New Leipzig school, a group of German artists who embraced a new form of representational painting. Although New Leipzig paintings are often narrative in nature, some present moody, dreamlike, romanticized, or spatially distorted landscapes, often in strong but faded colors. David Schnell's *Planks* (2005), for example, presents a view of a landscape through gaps in the planks of a structure that appears to be a barn or a covered bridge, providing only a distorted glimpse of the outside world.

Today's landscape painters create works both monumental and miniscule, using nearly every style that has been developed through the ages. Many of today's artists reinterpret old styles, merging them with their own ways of seeing and representing the world to speak to today's viewers. Others turn away from the styles of the past to portray their own unique visions, as have artists through the ages. The natural world has changed much in the past two millennia—as have the ways in which painters have depicted it. Through it all, landscape artists have maintained the ability to show us the imagined and the real, the ideal and the sublime, the emotional and the abstract, in the world around us.

PLANKS, BY DAVID SCHNELL

APPRECIATING ART

Christina's World (1948)

Andrew Wyeth, American (1917–2009)

32-1/4 x 47-3/4 inches (81.9 x 121.3 cm)

During Wyeth's time, much of modern art was moving toward less realistic portrayals of the natural world. Rejecting the style of the abstract artists, Wyeth turned to a style known as magic realism, presenting scenes from everyday life in new, unexpected ways and investing them with a sense of mystery and wonder— giving them an almost romantic feeling.

Christina's World is Wyeth's most famous painting. Based on the scenery around Wyeth's summer home in Cushing, Maine, the scene looks almost as if it could be a photograph (although Wyeth rearranged some of the elements of the real-life location). The artist pays close attention to the smallest details, down to individual blades of grass and strands of hair. Using a limited palette of earthy tones in tempera—rather than oil—paint, Wyeth creates subtle effects of light and shadow beneath the muted sky. The distant house looks rustic and worn, as much a part of the treeless landscape as the grass of the fields. The work is painted from an unusual angle, looking up from the bottom of a hill toward a high horizon. The viewer sees from the perspective of the girl on the hillside, who is almost engulfed by the landscape. Stricken with **polio**, she leans toward, but is unable to climb to, the top. The gentle colors, unique perspective, and quiet lighting of the scene imbue the work with a sense of longing and melancholy—a new type of poetry in paint.

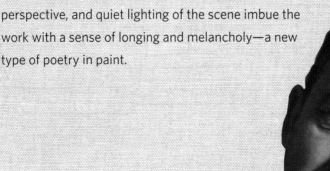

Glossary

abstract—relating to art that does not seek to represent an object or scene but focuses instead on form and design, often with no recognizable content

airbrushing—painting with a pencil-shaped device that sprays small drops of paint onto a surface to complete highly detailed work

contemporary—living or existing at the same time as someone or something else

divine—having to do with God, gods, or goddesses

Flanders—a region in northwestern Europe, including parts of present-day Belgium, France, and the Netherlands

genre—a category in which an artistic work can be classified on the basis of style, technique, or subject matter

illuminated manuscripts—handwritten books, often about religious subjects, created during the Middle Ages and adorned with decorations and small illustrations

linear perspective—a technique that allows artists to represent depth on a flat surface by making parallel lines come together as they near the horizon

mosaics—pictures made by adhering small pieces of colored tile, glass, or stone onto a surface, such as a wall or floor

pigment—a substance, usually a powder, that can be mixed with oil or water to give paint its color

polio—a viral disease that affects the brain and spinal cord, often leading to paralysis of specific muscle groups and deformity

relief—a work of art on which the figures or forms are raised above the surface

secular—not having to do with religion

stylized—designed to fit the rules of a particular style rather than to imitate nature

subconscious—the part of a person's mind that holds thoughts or memories of which he or she is unaware

symbols—objects that stand for something else, often an abstract idea, such as love or purity

symmetrical—containing elements of similar size, shape, or composition on either side of an imaginary dividing line through the center of a picture in order to maintain a feeling of balance

tempera—a type of paint created by mixing pigments with water and egg yolk or other substances

Virgin Mary—the mother of Jesus

West—the part of the world that includes Europe and North and South America, where culture has been influenced by ancient Greek and Roman civilizations, as well as Christianity

Selected Bibliography

Bazarov, Konstantin. *Landscape Painting*. New York: Mayflower Books, 1981.

Büttner, Nils. *Landscape Painting: A History*. Translated by Russell Stockman. New York: Abbeville Press Publishers, 2006.

Carli, Enzo. *The Landscape in Art: From 3000 B.C. to Today*. Edited by Mia Cinotti. New York: William Morrow and Company, 1980.

Hartt, Frederick, and David G. Wilkins. *History of Italian Renaissance Art*. New York: Harry N. Abrams, 2003.

Hollingsworth, Mary. *Art in World History*. 2 vols. Armonk, N.Y.: Sharpe Reference, 2004.

Janson, H. W., and Anthony F. Janson. *History of Art*. New York: Harry N. Abrams, 2001.

Sturgis, Alexander, and Hollis Clayson, eds. *Understanding Paintings: Themes in Art Explored and Explained*. New York: Watson-Guptill Publications, 2000.

Wood, Christopher. *Albrecht Altdorfer and the Origins of Landscape*. Chicago: University of Chicago Press, 1993.

Most of the paintings referenced in this book can be viewed online. By running an Internet image search using the names of paintings and artists, many works can be quickly located and viewed at the Web sites of various museums and online art galleries.

Index

abstract art 5, 37–38, 41, 45
altarpieces 9
Altdorfer, Albrecht 19–20
    Danube Landscape near Regensburg 19
    St. George and the Dragon 19–20
ancient Greek art 5, 9, 20, 26
ancient Roman art 5, 9, 26
atmospheric perspective 19
automatic painting 38
Baroque art 20, 22
Bellini, Giovanni 14, 15
    St. Francis in the Desert **14**, 15
Book of Kells **6**, **7**
Braque, Georges 33
    Houses at L'Estaque 33
Bruegel, Pieter (the Elder) 20, 21
    The Harvesters **21**
    Haymaking 20
    Hunters in the Snow 20
    The Seasons 20
Byzantine art 5, 6
Catholic Church 5
Cézanne, Paul 34, 35
    Mont Sainte-Victoire Seen from the Bibémus Quarry
        34, 35
Cole, Thomas 29–30
    The Oxbow 29–30
Constable, John 28–29
    The Hay Wain **28–29**, 29
Cubist art 33, 35, 37
da Vinci, Leonardo 9–11
    The Last Supper **10–11**
Dali, Salvador 38, 39
    The Font **39**
Danube school 20
Dove, Arthur G. 36, 37–38
    Sails **36**
Dürer, Albrecht 20
emotional themes 20, 26, 28, 38
environmental art 41
Estes, Richard 42, 42-43
    Lee (Corner Window) 42
Expressionist art 5
Fauvist art 33, 35
Frankenthaler, Helen 40, 41
    Mountains and Sea **40**, 41
frescoes 5, 9, 12, 16
Friedrich, Caspar David 28
    Monk by the Sea 28
Giorgione 18, 19
    The Tempest **18**, 19
Giotto di Bondone 5, 8, 9
    The Annunciation **5**
    St. Francis Receiving the Stigmata **8**
Goldsworthy, Andy 41
    Maple Leaf Lines 41
Hudson River school 29
hyperrealist art 43
illuminated manuscripts 6
Impressionist art 30, 35
Katsushika Hokusai 24, 25
    The Great Wave at Kanagawa **24**, 25
    Thirty-Six Views of Mount Fuji 25

landscapes as property records 11
linear perspective 9, 20
Lorenzetti, Ambrogio 16
    Effects of Good Government on Town and Country 16
Lorrain, Claude 20, 22
    Seaport with the Embarkation of Saint Ursula 22
Maestà Altarpiece **4**
magic realist art 45
Magritte, René 38
Masaccio 9
Matisse, Henri 33, 35
    Joy of Life 33
Middle Ages 5–6, 9, 10
Monet, Claude 30, 31
    Impression, Sunrise 30, **31**
    Stack of Wheat (End of Day, Autumn) 30
    Stack of Wheat (End of Summer) 30
    Stack of Wheat (Sunset, Snow Effect) 30
mosaics 5
natural themes 6, 9, 11, 15, 20, 26, 28, 29, 30, 35, 37, 41
Neoclassical art 26
New Leipzig school 43
oil paint 12, 15, 19, 28, 30
Ortelius, Abraham 20
outdoor painting 30, 35
Patinir, Joachim 20
    Landscape with the Flight into Egypt 20
photography 41–42, 43
photorealist art 37, 41–42, 43
Picasso, Pablo 33, 35
    House in a Garden 33
Pollock, Jackson 38, 41
Realist art 5
religious themes 5, 6, 9, 10, 12, 15, 19, 20
Renaissance 9–10, 15, 16
Rococo art 26
Romantic art 26, 28–29
Rothko, Mark 41
Schnell, David 42, 43
    Planks **42–43**, 43
Smithson, Robert 41
    Spiral Jetty 41
Surrealist art 37, 38
"The Surrealist Manifesto" 38
symbolism 6, 10, 15
tapestries 5
Tawaraya Sōtatsu 22–23
    Waves at Matsushima **22–23**, 23
tempera paint 15, 19, 45
ukiyo-e 25
Ulysses and Circes **12–13**
van Eyck, Jan 17, 19
    The Virgin and Child with Chancellor Rolin **17**, 19
van Gogh, Vincent 2, 30, 32, 33
    Harvest in Provence **32**, 33
    Wheatfield with Crows 33
    Wheatfield with Reaper **2**
van Ruisdael, Jacob 22–23
    The Jewish Cemetery 22
    View of Haarlem 22–23
wall paintings 5
Watteau, Jean-Antoine 26, 27
    An Embarrassing Proposal **27**
    Landscape with Waterfall **27**
    Pilgrimage to Cythera 26
Wyeth, Andrew 44, 45
    Christina's World **44**, 45
Yamato-e 6